Contents

Chapter	Page
1. "A Principle Within"	5
2. God's Gift to You	14
3. A Good Conscience	24
4. A Weak Conscience	33
5. A Strong Conscience	44
6. An Evil Conscience	54
7. Conscience and Ministry	64
8. Conscience and Government	74

"Conscience" in the New Testament

John 8:9
Acts 23:1; 24:16
Romans 2:15; 9:1; 13:5
I Corinthians 8:7,10,12; 10:25,27,28,29
II Corinthians 1:12; 4:2; 5:11
I Timothy 1:5,19; 3:9; 4:2
II Timothy 1:3
Titus 1:15
Hebrews 9:9,14; 10:2,22; 13:18
I Peter 2:19; 3:16,21

MEET YOUR CONSCIENCE

by Warren W. Wiersbe
General Director
Back to the Bible Broadcast

A
BACK TO THE BIBLE
PUBLICATION
LINCOLN, NE. 68501

VICTOR
BOOKS a division of SP Publications, Inc.
WHEATON. ILLINOIS 60187

Offices also in
Whitby, Ontario, Canada
Amersham-on-the-Hill, Bucks, England

65,000 printed to date—1983
(5-1909—65M—43)
ISBN 0-8474-6506-3

All Scripture quotations are from *The New Scofield Reference Bible.*

Printed in the United States of America

Chapter 1

"A Principle Within"

"I want a principle within / Of watchful, godly fear."

When Charles Wesley wrote those words, he was expressing a truth concerning conscience. The German philosopher Immanuel Kant wrote: "Two things fill the mind with ever-increasing wonder and awe . . . : the starry heavens above me and the moral law within me."

Something within the heart of every person *approves* when we do right and *accuses* when we do wrong, and that something is conscience.

The word "conscience" is found 32 times in the New Testament (King James Version) and was used 21 times by the Apostle Paul. If we are going to be successful in our Christian lives, we must understand what conscience is and how it functions.

I want to discuss two topics related to conscience. First, the *definition:* What is conscience? Second, the *description:* How is conscience pictured in the Word of God? If we understand what conscience is and how it functions, it can change our lives.

Definition of Conscience

You cannot escape conscience. You have to live with your conscience. You can argue with your conscience. You can defile your conscience. You can harden your conscience. But you will never get rid of your conscience. It may misfunction because you force it to misfunction, but it will always be there. Sad is the life where conscience does not work the way God wants it to work!

What is conscience? The word "conscience" in our English language comes from two Latin words. *Com* means "with" or "together," and *scio* means "I know." From the Latin, our English word "conscience" means "to know with" or "to know together." To know with what? To know with ourselves and to know within ourselves. Conscience is that inner knowledge that helps me to know myself.

The Greek word used in the New Testament, *suneidesis,* means exactly the same thing. It comes from two Greek words, *sun* and *oida,* that mean "to know with."

In New Testament days the word "conscience" was not a strange word. It was used by the Greek people in their everyday conversation. It meant "the pain that you feel when you do wrong." That's a good definition, isn't it?

An American Indian who was a Christian said, "In my heart there is an arrowhead with three points to it. If I do wrong, the arrowhead turns, and it cuts me. If I do wrong too much, I wear out the points and it doesn't hurt me quite so much." But when the pain is gone, watch out!

Conscience is that inner faculty that indicates to us whether our actions are right or wrong, according to the standards within our hearts. Oswald Chambers gave a good definition of conscience: "The conscience is that innate faculty in a man's spirit that attaches itself to the highest that the man knows." Conscience is not the law; conscience bears witness to the law. Conscience is not the standard; conscience bears witness to the standard. In different parts of the world there are different standards.

Let me illustrate this. When the British took over India as part of their empire, they found some practices that simply had to be abolished. One of these practices was to burn the widow of a deceased man on the funeral pyre. The British issued a law abolishing this practice.

One of the religious leaders among the Indian people came to a British leader and said, "Our conscience tells us that the widow must be burned." And he responded, "And our conscience tells us that if you do it, we'll hang you!" That gives the difference, doesn't it?

Conscience can guide us aright if we have the right standard. Everyone has experienced this. If you cheat on an examination, tell a lie or do something you simply should not do, your conscience bothers you. Something down inside keeps reminding you that you should not have done that. That's conscience. Of course, some people have so abused their conscience that it doesn't bother them any-more; for these people we can only feel pity.

When Adam and Eve sinned against God, they hid. Do you know why? Their consciences were bothering them. They were afraid.

When David cut off part of Saul's skirt while Saul was asleep, David's heart smote him (see I Sam. 24:1-6). That's conscience. He knew that he should not have done this to the king of Israel. Even though Saul was not a godly man, he was the king. David could not respect the man, but he had to respect the office. His conscience bothered him when he treated the king that way.

Proverbs 28:1 says, "The wicked flee when no man pursueth." That's conscience. We read that Herod, when he heard about the miracles Jesus was doing, thought that John the Baptist had come back to life again. His conscience was bothering him. "John, whom I have beheaded; he is raised from the dead" (Mark 6:16). That's conscience.

Two Descriptions of Conscience

Let's look at two beautiful descriptions of con-science in the Bible. The Apostle Paul gave us one of them in Romans 2:14,15, and the Lord Jesus gave us another in Matthew 6:22,23. Paul compared con-science to an inner witness, an inner judge.

Paul's Description

"For when the Gentiles, who have not the law, do by nature the things contained in the law, these, having not the law, are a law unto themselves; who

8

show the work of the law written in their hearts, their conscience also bearing witness, and their thoughts the meanwhile accusing or else excusing one another" (Rom. 2:14,15).

The Gentiles were never given the Law. The Law was given to the Jews. But the Gentiles have the *work* of the Law written in their hearts. Notice that Paul did not say they have *the Law* written in their hearts. That doesn't happen until you're saved. When you're saved, then the Holy Spirit begins to write God's law in your heart and you know right from wrong. But even unsaved people can know right from wrong because their conscience bears witness.

In the inner man is a courtroom. A judge sits at the bench, and that judge is also the witness and the jury! That whole "group" in the courtroom is known as conscience. The judge does not make the law, he applies the law. When you and I do something right, then our conscience says, "That's good! That's good!" It does not accuse, it approves. When we do something wrong, that inner judge, that inner witness, says to us, "You are wrong! You are wrong!" And it hurts.

Conscience, you see, is judicial. Conscience does not *pass* the law. Conscience does not *make* the law. Conscience *bears witness* to the law.

You and I can remember when we were little children, even before we understood all that was involved in ethics and morals, that when we did something wrong, something would bother us down inside. That was conscience.

Paul told us that conscience is an inner witness that indicates whether we have done right or wrong. "Their thoughts the meanwhile accusing or else excusing one another" (v. 15). Paul told us that *everyone* has this faculty. This is not something we have to develop. It is there. God has given every person a conscience.

Let me remind you once again, conscience is not the law. Conscience functions according to the law that we have. If we are given a standard and if that standard is not right, conscience will still work according to that standard. The important thing is to have the *right* standard so that our conscience can work the way God wants it to work.

Jesus' Description

This leads us to what our Lord Jesus said in Matthew 6:22,23: "The lamp of the body is the eye; if, therefore, thine eye be healthy, thy whole body shall be full of light. But if thine eye be evil, thy whole body shall be full of darkness. If, therefore, the light that is in thee be darkness, how great is that darkness!"

Paul compared conscience to a witness; Jesus compared conscience to a window. The window does not manufacture the light—the window lets the light in. You and I have this inner window through which God wants to shine His light. If that window gets dirty, less light can come in. Imagine the judge sitting in the courtroom at his desk. On this desk is the Law of God. Through the window comes the light, and that light shines upon the Law.

10

Now, as that window gets dirtier, less light shines upon that Law, and that Law is less visible. If the window gets completely covered with dirt, it's impossible to see the Law. This is how conscience functions. That's why we say conscience witnesses to the highest standard we have. The highest standard, of course, is the Word of God.

Jesus said conscience is like your eye. The eye does not manufacture light—the eye lets light in. When the light comes into our lives, it gives us guidance. But suppose that every time we do something wrong, the window gets dirtier until finally we have sinned so much that the window is completely covered with dirt. The light cannot come through, and so we are left in the darkness!

It's a terrible thing when light turns into darkness. Our Lord did not say that the light disappears but that *the light turns into darkness!* What should lead us in the right path leads us in the wrong path. The Bible calls this an evil conscience.

Some people, if they do good, are bothered by it; but if they do evil, they are happy. That is an evil conscience. There are those who call evil "good" and good "evil." That's an evil conscience. Your conscience is like a window, and the window lets in the light. Don't let the light become darkness!

When a person becomes a Christian, God cleanses the conscience. No matter what we have done, no matter how we have sinned, God cleanses our conscience. And when the conscience is cleansed, then the light of God's Word can penetrate to our inner being. As we read the Word of

God, we discover that God has certain standards. Some things are right, and some things are wrong. We must not do or say or be involved in some things. As we obey God's Word, then the window gets cleaner and cleaner, and more light shines in.

Have you ever wondered why some Christians have more discernment than others? Have you ever wondered why some saints of God always seem to know where they're supposed to go and what they're supposed to do? They seem to have an inner compass that directs them. This is their conscience. The Holy Spirit wants to work with your conscience to guide you and to help you grow in the Christian life. This is why conscience is such a wonderful blessing, because a good conscience can help you live a good Christian life.

We're going to discover that there are many different kinds of consciences. Some people have a weak conscience. Some have a strong conscience. Some have a defiled conscience. Some have an evil conscience. You may be saying right now, "My conscience is really in trouble. It doesn't bother me anymore. I'm doing things today that, if I had done them a year ago, would have bothered me all night! But I don't worry anymore." This is not good, but God can cleanse your conscience.

Suppose that every time you sinned, you lost a little bit of your vision. How much sinning would you do? You say, "Oh, I wouldn't do much sinning! I wouldn't want to lose my sight!" That's true. But we do this to our conscience all the time.

Your conscience is a marvelous servant. It was

designed to work for you and with you. When a person works toward having a good conscience, he becomes a good Christian, has a good witness for the Lord Jesus Christ and enjoys the good blessings God has for him. He never has to vascillate from one thing to another, asking, "Do I go here? Do I go there? What does God want me to do?" It's a beautiful experience to have a healthy conscience.

If something is wrong right now with your conscience, confess it to the Lord. Make it right with Him. Don't begin the day or the activities of life with a conscience that's defiled. The Lord Jesus Christ can forgive you and cleanse you and give you a healthy conscience. Then you can learn how to exercise that conscience and live to the glory of God.

Chapter 2

God's Gift to You

Your conscience is important, and you should be very careful what you do to it and with it. Let me give you eight reasons why your conscience is important.

Conscience Is God's Gift

Your conscience is important because *it is God's gift to you.* You were made "in the image of God" (Gen. 1:27). Being made in God's image means we have a mind to think with, a heart to feel with and a will to decide with. Our basic nature is spiritual. A person is not just a body; he is fundamentally spiritual. Saint Augustine said, "Thou hast made us for Thyself, and the heart of man is restless until it finds its rest in Thee." One aspect of this image of God in people is the ability to distinguish right from wrong. Romans 2:14,15 tells us that people have a conscience. It's God's gift to them.

Scientists are trying to discover where conscience comes from. A number of false views about the origin of conscience have developed. Some say that conscience comes *from behind us*—it's a part of evolution. As man evolved over the centuries,

14

conscience evolved with him. And yet Darwin in his book *The Descent of Man* said this: "Of all the differences between man and the lower animals, the moral sense, or conscience, is by far the most important." Even Darwin couldn't explain where conscience came from.

Conscience is not the by-product of evolution; it did not come from behind us. Nor did conscience come *from around us.* I hear people saying that conscience is merely the total of all the standards of the society around you.

The philosopher Schopenhauer said that conscience consisted of "one-fifth the fear of man, one-fifth superstition, one-fifth prejudice, one-fifth vanity and one-fifth custom." In other words, your conscience is a sort of "tossed salad" that you put together from the society around you.

Society does help to give us standards, but society does not give us the conscience. We have learned that conscience is that faculty *that responds to the standards we have.* Conscience does not manufacture the standards, and the standards do not manufacture the conscience. Conscience is the window that lets in the light—it doesn't manufacture the light. While people have different customs and standards in different parts of the world, conscience still functions the same way no matter where you go.

Conscience does not come from behind us, and conscience does not come from around us. Nor does conscience come *from within us.* Many psychiatrists want us to believe that we have manufactured our own conscience—it's the by-product of the way Mother raised us and the way Father disciplined us. I disagree with all these explanations. I think that conscience is the gift of God. According to the Word of God, conscience came *from above us*. Conscience is a universal phenomenon. Conscience is found everywhere in the world; therefore, it must have a common source, and that common source is God. God has put within the hearts of people this wonderful faculty called conscience. Therefore, you must be careful how you treat your conscience because it is God's gift to you.

Conscience Guides Our Conduct

There's a second reason why conscience is important: *Conscience guides our conduct.* I've heard people say, "Let your conscience be your guide," and to some degree this is good advice. It's important, however, for conscience to have the right guide, the right standard to follow.

In Acts 24:16 we read the words of the Apostle Paul: "In this do I exercise myself, to have always a conscience void of offense toward God, and toward men." Paul admitted that his conscience needed *exercise*. If conscience is not exercised, it will begin to function in the wrong way. It will no longer be "void of offense toward God, and toward men." But when conscience is functioning properly, it can guide us.

The Holy Spirit wants to use your conscience. In Romans 9:1 Paul wrote that *his conscience was bearing witness* in the Spirit of God. The Holy Spirit uses the Word of God to show us the will of God, and our conscience is involved in this process. If your conscience is functioning the way it should, then you have a compass to direct you, a light to guide you and a law to give you wisdom in the Christian life.

Conscience Strengthens for Service

Conscience is important because it is God's gift to you and because it can guide your conduct. Third, conscience is important because *it strengthens you for Christian service.*

We read in I Timothy 1:5: "Now the end of the commandment is love out of a pure heart, and of a good conscience, and of faith unfeigned [sincere faith, not hypocritical faith]." The purpose of the ministry of the Word of God is that I might have love from a pure heart, that I might have a good conscience and that I might have sincere faith that is not hypocritical.

First Timothy 1:19 says, "Holding faith, and a good conscience, which some, having put away concerning faith, have made shipwreck." When you start playing around with your conscience, you're heading for shipwreck. Conscience is the compass that guides us. When you don't follow that compass or when you try to change the compass, you're going to end up shipwrecked.

In I Timothy 3:9 Paul wrote that the deacons should hold "the mystery of the faith in a pure conscience." So conscience is connected very definitely to our ministry and our service as Christians.

In II Corinthians 4:2 Paul wrote: "But [we] have renounced the hidden things of dishonesty, not walking in craftiness, nor handling the word of God deceitfully, but by manifestation of the truth commending ourselves to every man's conscience in the sight of God."

Second Corinthians 5:11 says, "Knowing, therefore, the terror of the Lord, we persuade men; but we are made manifest unto God, and I trust also are made manifest in your consciences."

In his ministry Paul was very careful to have a clear conscience and to minister to the consciences of others. Conscience is important because it strengthens us for Christian service. When your conscience is clear, you can face any enemy.

Conscience Strengthens Fellowship

Conscience also *strengthens our Christian fellowship.* We're going to discover from Romans 14 and 15 and from I Corinthians 8, 9 and 10 that some people have a strong conscience and some people have a weak conscience. Those with a weak conscience often create problems in the fellowship. Sometimes those who have a strong conscience do too, but usually it's the other way around.

Some in the Roman assemblies had a weak conscience, and they would not eat meat. Some in the Corinthian church had a strong conscience; they not only ate meat, but they also ate it at the idol temples and participated in idolatrous feasts. Paul wrote to those people and explained what it meant

18

to have a weak conscience and what it meant to have a strong conscience.

You want to become the kind of Christian who has a strong conscience. A strong conscience does not give you the privilege of sinning! The person with a strong conscience claims the privileges and the freedoms that we have in the Word of God, enjoys these privileges and these freedoms but never uses them to hurt others. We would solve a great many problems in our churches if we'd learn how to have a strong conscience. People are divided over everything under the sun. We Christians don't have enough faith to accept the truth of the Word of God and act upon it. Sometimes strong Christians don't know how to accept weak Christians and help them grow up in the Lord. Conscience strengthens our fellowship.

Conscience Encourages Witnessing

There is a fifth reason why your conscience is important: *It encourages your witness.* When you have a strong conscience and a good conscience, you aren't afraid to face the problems and difficulties of life. You see them as opportunities for witnessing.

First Peter 2:19 says, "For this is thankworthy, if a man for conscience toward God endure grief, suffering wrongfully." Anybody can suffer when he's done something wrong—that doesn't take much grace. But when you've done something *right* and you suffer for it, that's something else. What takes you through that suffering? A good conscience.

19

When your conscience is right between you and God, it makes little difference what people say about you or do to you.

First Peter 3:15,16 says, "But sanctify the Lord God in your hearts, and be ready always to give an answer to every man that asketh you a reason of the hope that is in you, with meekness and fear, having a good conscience, that, whereas they speak evil of you, as of evildoers, they may be ashamed that falsely accuse your good manner of life [behavior] in Christ."

A good conscience encourages your witness. Nothing will shut your mouth like a conscience that convicts you. When we know we've done something wrong, when there's something between us and the Lord, we're not very good witnesses, are we?

Conscience Helps in Prayer

There's a sixth reason why we should have a good conscience: *It helps us in prayer.* First John 3:19-22 says, "And by this we know that we are of the truth, and shall assure our hearts before him. For if our heart condemn us, God is greater than our heart, and knoweth all things. Beloved, if our heart condemn us not, then have we confidence toward God. And whatever we ask, we receive of him, because we keep his commandments, and do those things that are pleasing in his sight."

If when I kneel to pray, my conscience convicts me, I have to get it straightened out before I can talk to God. If I come to the Lord in prayer, and something is wrong in my life, my conscience will tell me about it. It's wonderful to be able to pray in the will of God and not be accused by our conscience.

The psalmist said, "If I regard iniquity in my heart, the Lord will not hear me" (Ps. 66:18). Conscience helps us in our praying. As we face the Lord, if we have a good conscience, a conscience void of offense toward God and toward others, then we can pray effectively.

Jesus talked about this in the Sermon on the Mount. He said, "If you're going to the altar to offer your sacrifice and remember that there's something between you and your brother, leave your sacrifice. First go and be reconciled with your brother. Then come and offer your sacrifice" (see Matt. 5:23,24).

Conscience Affects Citizenship

There's a seventh reason why we should pay attention to our conscience and be careful how we treat it: *It affects our citizenship.*

Are there times when Christians should not obey the government? In Romans 13 we're told that every person should be subject to the higher powers because those higher powers are ordained of God. So we should obey the law because God has established government. We should obey the law because government has established punishment. If we don't obey, we'll be punished.

But in Romans 13:5 Paul said, "Wherefore, ye must needs be subject, not only for wrath but also for conscience sake." What is a conscientious objector? Is there such a thing in the Word of God

21

as civil disobedience? If your conscience is functioning as it should, it helps you know when to obey and when not to obey the law.

Suppose you are told not to witness. Suppose, like Daniel, you are told not to pray. Suppose, like those Hebrew midwives, you are told to murder babies. What will you do? Conscience helps us in our citizenship. It helps us to be good citizens and to use our citizenship to the glory of God.

Conscience Helps Build Character

The eighth reason why we should care for our conscience is this: *It helps us to build character.* Hebrews 5:13,14 says, "For everyone that useth milk is unskillful in the word of righteousness; for he is a babe. But solid food belongeth to them that are of full age, even those who by reason of use have their senses exercised to discern both good and evil." The writer was talking here about growing and maturing in the Christian life. If you do not use your faculties, they could become useless. If a person ties his right arm to his body and doesn't use it, it will atrophy.

Our spiritual senses function in a similar way. If we don't exercise our spiritual senses, then we never learn how to discern between good and evil, and then we don't grow in Christian character. It is important for us to build up our conscience—to have a good conscience, a pure conscience, a conscience void of offense—because this helps us to build Christian character.

I trust I have convinced you from these eight

reasons that your conscience is important. We cannot afford to fool around with, or toy with, conscience. Conscience is God's gift to you. It can guide your conduct, strengthen you for service, strengthen you in Christian fellowship, encourage you in your witnessing, help you in your praying, give you guidance concerning your citizenship and ultimately help you to build your character. This is why Charles Wesley wrote in that hymn: "I want a principle within / Of watchful, godly fear." That principle is conscience.

If you don't know Jesus Christ personally, trust Him as your Saviour. He will cleanse your conscience, and then it will help build your life to the glory of God.

Chapter 3

A Good Conscience

Conscience is one of the servants God has given us to help us in our Christian life. The New Testament speaks of many different kinds of conscience: a *pure* conscience as well as a *defiled* conscience, a *good* conscience and an *evil* conscience, a *strong* conscience and a *weak* conscience.

We want to focus on the characteristics of a good conscience. The Apostle Paul said in Acts 24:16, "And in this do I exercise myself, to have always a conscience void of offense toward God, and toward men."

What are the characteristics of a good conscience? It has at least three characteristics.

A Good Conscience Is Effective

First, *a good conscience is effective.* It works. If you had an automobile that didn't run, you wouldn't call it a good automobile. You'd just call it an automobile that's not running. If you have a conscience that is not operating effectively, you could not call it a good conscience. A good conscience is one that actually works in our lives.

Keeps Us on Course

A good conscience effectively keeps us on course. "As I besought thee to abide still at Ephesus, when I went into Macedonia, that thou mightest charge some that they teach no other doctrine, neither give heed to fables and endless genealogies, which minister questions rather than godly edifying which is in faith, so do. Now the end [object] of the commandment is love out of a pure heart, and of a good conscience, and of faith unfeigned, from which some, having swerved, have turned aside unto vain jangling" (I Tim. 1:3-6).

Paul warned Timothy to stick to the doctrines of the Word of God. They help us develop a good conscience, and a good conscience will keep us on course.

Verse 6 uses the phrase "have turned aside." This phrase means they have missed the mark, they have swerved, they have gone off course. You see, God has a course for each of us, and we had better stay on that course. If we don't stay on course, we won't achieve the purposes God has for us. A good conscience keeps us from going off course to fables and foolish arguments.

In my ministry of more than 30 years now, I have seen many people go off course in their Christian walk. They simply have not been on target. They've gotten off on some detour, some trivial thing. Some of them, unfortunately, have gotten off into sin and unbelief. A good conscience will keep you from doing this.

Helps Us Be Victorious

Second, *a good conscience will help you to have victory.* First Timothy 1:18,19 says, "This charge I commit unto thee, son Timothy, according to the prophecies which pointed to thee, that thou by them mightest war a good warfare, holding faith, and a good conscience, which some, having put away concerning faith, have made shipwreck."

First you go off course, and then you wreck the ship. We are in a battle. We must fight a good warfare. Some warfare is bad, but this is a good warfare, a warfare against the world, the flesh and the Devil. Those who have faith and a good conscience can fight the battle and win the victory. Nothing gives you greater courage as you face the battles of life than a good conscience, one that is functioning well in your life.

Timothy had some battles in Ephesus where he pastored. That would not be an easy place to pastor. Ministers write to me or phone me and say, "Brother Wiersbe, I am in a rough place!" There are no easy places. Wherever you lift the banner of Jesus Christ, the Devil is going to fight you, and if he can, he will use the members of the church to do it! If you hold on to faith and a good conscience, you can wage the good warfare.

Helps Us Be Honest

A good conscience not only keeps us on course and helps us to have victory, but *a good conscience will also help us to be honest.* Hebrews 13:18 says,

26

"Pray for us; for we trust we have a good conscience, in all things willing to live honestly." The word translated "honestly" means "beautifully, seemingly, fittingly." The Christian life is to be a beautiful life. Christians should not create problems— they should solve problems. Usually a Christian doesn't create problems, he reveals them. The problems were already there. But if you have a good conscience, you will be able to live an honest life, a beautiful life. People will look at you and say, "There is something about him or her that is really lovely."

It's unfortunate when Christians don't pay their bills. It's unfortunate when Christians have a bad reputation in the business community. If a person has a good conscience, he will live honestly, pay his bills and keep his promises. He will be true to his contracts because his conscience will help him to live honestly.

Keeps Us Witnessing

In I Peter 3:14-17 we discover that *a good conscience is effective to keep us witnessing.* "But and if ye suffer for righteousness' sake, happy are ye: and be not afraid of their terror, neither be troubled, but sanctify the Lord God in your hearts, and be ready always to give an answer to every man that asketh you a reason of the hope that is in you, with meekness and fear, having a good conscience, that, whereas they speak evil of you, as of evildoers, they may be ashamed that falsely accuse your good manner of life [behavior] in Christ. For it is better, if

27

the will of God be so, that ye suffer for well-doing than for evil-doing."

Peter was writing to people who were being falsely accused. That's a hard thing to experience. They were being accused of saying and doing things that they had not said and done. How were they to prove that these accusations were wrong? Were they supposed to go to court? Were they supposed to hold a protest meeting? No, he simply said, "Be ready to witness."

Obstacles can become opportunities. When people are making trouble for you, it is an opportunity to witness if you have a good conscience. If you've done evil, your conscience will rebuke you and convict you, but if you are doing good, your conscience will strengthen you. There is nothing like a good conscience to keep you strong when people are lying about you.

A good conscience is an effective conscience. It keeps us on course, keeps us victorious, keeps us honest and keeps us witnessing when the going is tough. The person who abandons a good conscience begins to swerve off course and to move toward the dangerous reefs of life, and before long he is shipwrecked.

This is what happened to King Saul. King Saul began to play with his conscience, and before long he got off course. Then he lost the victory and began to lie and make excuses. Before long he was dead. It is an important thing to have a good conscience. A good conscience is effective.

A Good Conscience Is Enlightened

The second characteristic of a good conscience is this: *A good conscience is enlightened.* A good conscience is taught by the Word of God and guided by the Spirit of God.

The Lord Jesus compared conscience to a window that lets in light. Matthew 6:22,23 says, "The lamp of the body is the eye; if, therefore, thine eye be healthy, thy whole body shall be full of light. But if thine eye be evil, thy whole body shall be full of darkness. If, therefore, the light that is in thee be darkness, how great is that darkness!"

Conscience is a window that lets in the light, and the more light you have from the Word of God, the better your conscience is going to function. Conscience attaches itself to the highest standard that the person knows. As we grow in our Christian life, our standard gets higher and higher. When we first meet the Lord, we have many things to learn. As the light begins to shine into our hearts, we see the cobwebs and the dust, and we begin to clean things up. The more knowledge you have about God and the more knowledge you have about the grace of God, the better your conscience will function. This is why we must read the Word of God, exhort one another and seek the light from the Holy Spirit.

In I Corinthians 8 Paul made it clear that *knowledge* and *conscience* go together. The consciences of some people don't bother them because they don't have the knowledge that should enlighten their consciences. Some people do not have any light; they have darkness—the darkness of superstition and ignorance.

When John Knox was preaching the Gospel in Scotland and seeking to reform the church, Queen Mary, who had a different belief, opposed him. She said to him one day, "My conscience is not so." John Knox replied to Queen Mary, "Conscience, Madam, requires knowledge, and I fear that right knowledge you have none."

A Good Conscience Is Exercised

A good conscience is effective. A good conscience is enlightened. And third, *a good conscience is exercised.*

Paul told Felix, "And in this do I exercise myself, to have always a conscience void of offense toward God, and toward men" (Acts 24:16). Our conscience, like our muscles, must be exercised. If our conscience lies dormant and is not exercised, then it becomes an evil conscience.

Hebrews 5:13,14 describes this: "For everyone that useth milk is unskillful in the word of righteousness; for he is a babe. But solid food belongeth to them that are of full age, even those who by reason of use have their senses exercised to discern both good and evil."

Each of our physical senses can be exercised to an amazing degree of proficiency. People can be taught to hear better or to see clearer. Some people have an amazing sense of touch. Even the sense of taste can be trained to a marvelous degree of proficiency. In the same way our spiritual senses—our spiritual sight, our spiritual hearing, our spiritual taste—must be exercised if we're going to have discernment, and this involves conscience.

Conscience must be exercised, otherwise it cannot be a good conscience. And you exercise your conscience when you obey the Word of God, when you do the things God tells you to do. Just as a musician develops skill as he practices his music, just as a cook develops skill as she continually prepares meals or an artist develops skill the more he paints—so the Christian develops a keen sensitivity about what is right and wrong as he obeys the Word of God. A good conscience is one that is exercised.

The Greek word (*apeiros*) translated "unskillful" in Hebrews 5:13 means "without experience." The Greek word (*gumnazo*) translated "exercise" in verse 14 gives us our English word "gymnasium." The Greeks were great believers in physical exercise. The writer of Hebrews is saying, "Just as you exercise your physical senses and your physical muscles, so you must exercise your spiritual senses and your conscience, for a good conscience is one that is exercised."

Do you have a good conscience? Is your conscience effective? Is it working? When you have done something wrong, does your conscience bother you? When you do something right and people oppose you, does your conscience strengthen you?

I trust that your conscience is an enlightened conscience and that you are growing in your knowledge of the Word of God. I trust you aren't living by custom or tradition but by the truth of the Word of God.

It is thrilling when you are not only *walking* in the light of God's Word but also *carrying* the light with you wherever you go.

Do you have an exercised conscience? Or do you say, "Well, what difference does it make?" The only way to grow as a Christian, the only way to stand as a Christian, the only way to be effective as a Christian is to exercise your conscience and to grow toward maturity in the Lord. It's a wonderful thing to have a good conscience. Do everything you can to keep your conscience in good repair. Once a good conscience starts to fail, you're moving toward shipwreck.

May the Lord help us to have a good conscience.

Chapter 4

A Weak Conscience

The Apostle Paul devoted nearly five chapters in two of his letters to the problems caused by people who have a weak conscience: I Corinthians 8, 9 and 10 and Romans 14 and 15. God wants us to develop a strong conscience because Christians who have a weak conscience can create problems for themselves and for other believers. In fact, I am convinced that many of the divisions and dissensions in churches today and across the evangelical world are caused by people who have a weak conscience.

Let's consider this matter of a weak conscience by looking at three important topics.

Characteristics of a Weak Conscience

First, let's consider *the characteristics of a weak conscience*. How can I tell whether or not I am a Christian with a weak conscience? There are at least eight characteristics of the person with the weak conscience.

Saved and in the Church

First of all, he *is* saved. Let's make this very clear. He is saved, and second, he is in the church. In

Romans 14:1 Paul said, "Him that is weak in the faith receive ye, but not to doubtful disputations." In other words, this person is a Christian, and he is in the church. He's not supposed to be kept out of the church because he has a weak conscience.

Lacks Knowledge

Third, he lacks knowledge. In I Corinthians 8:7 we read these words: "However, there is not in every man that knowledge; for some with conscience of the idol unto this hour eat it [this food] as a thing offered unto an idol, and their conscience, being weak, is defiled."

The problem in the Corinthian church was "Should a Christian eat meat that's been offered on the altar of some idol?" The cheapest meat in Corinth was available from the butcher shops at the temples. The strong Christians said, "An idol is nothing, and meat offered to an idol is not defiled; so I'll buy that meat." The weak Christians said, "Oh, no! We were saved out of idolatry, and that meat has been defiled!" And so the weak Christians did not have enough knowledge to understand spiritual things. They were still living, as it were, in infancy, and they didn't realize that food itself is neither good nor bad in relation to the spiritual life.

Easily Wounded and Offended

A fourth characteristic is that the person with the weak conscience is easily wounded and offended. First Corinthians 8:12 says, "But when ye sin so against the brethren, and wound their weak conscience, ye sin against Christ." Romans 14:15 says, "But if thy brother be grieved with thy food, now walkest thou not in love. Destroy not him with thy food, for whom Christ died."

Unstable

The person with the weak conscience is very easily wounded, very easily offended, and he's bothered by the freedom practiced by those who have a strong conscience. This leads to the fifth characteristic: He's very unstable, and he stumbles very easily. Romans 14:13 says, "Let us not, therefore, judge one another any more; but judge this, rather: that no man put a stumbling block or an occasion to fall in his brother's way."

Little children who are immature stumble over the smallest things. But adults, who have learned how to walk and balance themselves, are not usually troubled by those things.

Critical of Others

A sixth characteristic of a person with a weak conscience is this: He is very critical of others. Romans 14:3,4 says, "Let not him that eateth despise him that eateth not; and let not him who eateth not judge him that eateth; for God hath received him. Who art thou that judgest another man's servant? To his own master he standeth or falleth. Yea, he shall be held up; for God is able to make him stand."

In the Roman church the problem was what you should eat and on what day you should honor God.

They had problems with diets and days. The weaker Christians said, "Oh, we cannot eat this meat! We cannot eat these things!" The stronger Christians said, "You can eat anything." The weak Christians said, "Certain days are very special, and we must commemorate these days." The stronger Christians said, "Every day is a good day if you're walking with the Lord." The result was a divided church because the weaker Christians were critical of the stronger Christians.

Legalistic

The Christian with the weak conscience is legalistic. He lives by rules and regulations because he fears freedom. He is like a child. A child enjoys being smothered by Mother's love—he enjoys the protection. Then one day Mother says, "OK, you're going off to school." The child says, "I don't want to go to school." So he runs home from school, or he hides when he should be going to school. Why? He's afraid of freedom. It's dangerous to cross the street; it's dangerous to be thrown into a crowd of people you don't know. Mature adults don't worry about that. In fact, as we mature in the Lord we are happy to have new experiences, to meet new people, to face new challenges.

The person with the weak conscience is legalistic. He follows many rules and regulations. Please understand, I am not opposing standards. Mature adults must have standards. There are some things we will not do because we know better. But that's not what we build our lives on. We have standards

36

because we love the Lord, because we love one another, because we've learned to appreciate the things that are good and holy and right. But the person with the weak conscience is very legalistic. He measures everybody else by his rules, and he is very easily offended if you do something different from the way he does it.

Confused Priorities

Finally, the person with the weak conscience has his priorities confused. He focuses on the externals and not on the internals and the eternals. Romans 14:17 says, "For the kingdom of God is not food and drink, but righteousness, and peace, and joy in the Holy Spirit." The weak saints have a list of rules and regulations concerning what to eat and what not to eat, where to go and where not to go. But Paul said that these external things are not the important things. They are the by-products of what God is doing in your heart. Therefore, don't get your priorities confused.

Some people have the idea that the person with the rigid rules and regulations is the one with the strong conscience, and the person who exercises freedom in the Lord has the weak conscience. But it's just the other way around! The person with the strong conscience is tolerant of the differences he sees in other people. The person with the strong conscience does not stumble or become easily offended because of what somebody says or does. The person with the weak conscience is the person who, when he sees one thing in a magazine that he doesn't like, cancels his subscription. The Christian with the weak conscience is the one who, when he hears a piece of music he doesn't like, either leaves the church or stops supporting the radio ministry. The person with the weak conscience is the one who, when the preacher uses a different translation from what he prefers, will not support that church any more. That person is not spiritual at all; he has a lot of growing to do.

The Cause of a Weak Conscience

This leads to our second topic: *What is the cause of a weak conscience?* Why are people in our churches easily offended, critical, unstable and legalistic? What causes this? I think basically it is lack of growth. I think these people are afraid of freedom. Perhaps they were raised this way. Some people are raised in very legalistic homes, and they don't have the confidence of the Lord in their lives. Some people need constant support. They have to be propped up to be assured. They are, in a word, like children.

It's one thing to be *childlike,* but it's quite another to be *childish.* It's a marvelous thing for a little baby to cling to Mother. It's a terrible thing for a 40-year-old man to cling to a set of rules and regulations. Basically it boils down to a lack of spiritual knowledge.

In I Corinthians 8 Paul made it very clear that knowledge, love and conscience go together. As we grow in knowledge and as we practice love, we grow in the Lord and develop a strong conscience.

Hebrews 5:12-14 pretty well summarizes this situation: "For when for the time ye ought to be teachers, ye have need that one teach you again the first principles of the oracles of God, and are become such as have need of milk, and not of solid food. For everyone that useth milk is unskillful in the word of righteousness; for he is a babe. But solid food belongeth to them that are of full age, even those who by reason of use have their senses exercised to discern both good and evil." In other words, when the child of God feeds on the Word of God (the food) and obeys the Lord (the exercise), then he grows. Conscience grows as it is exercised.

How do you hinder conscience from growing? Depend on other people to tell you what to say and do. Have a list of rules and regulations, some external standards (other than biblical standards) that guide you in making your decisions.

We have had the joy of raising four children. When they were little, we had to have rules and regulations. We had to say, "You *don't* go near the highway. You do not leave the back door open—the baby may fall down the stairs. You do not leave a knife on the table—the baby may pick it up and get hurt." But as the children grew older, flexibility moved into our home, and we started operating, not by rules and regulations but by love and principles.

We live by certain principles. We want our children to grow. We want them to be able to exercise discernment. We can't constantly be making their decisions for them. How terrible it would be if God

39

handed us a little rule book that told us what to watch on television, what to read in the newspapers and what to do here and what to do there. We would never grow. We would never exercise our muscles.

The cause of a weak conscience is lack of knowledge (the window is not letting in the light), lack of exercise and a fear of freedom. Some ministries keep people weak so that they might be able to manipulate them and make them do what they want them to do. My task as a minister of the Gospel is to help you grow, which leads us to our third topic.

The Cure for a Weak Conscience

What is the cure for a weak conscience? I'll tell you what the cure is not. It's not scolding, and it's not beating weak saints over the head!

If your little child is lying in bed saying, "Daddy, there's a bear under my bed," you know very well there's no bear under the bed. But scolding won't solve the problem. What do you do? You go in, you turn the light on, you put your arms around the child, you assure the child that Daddy and Mommy are there. After a while the child laughs and says, "Well, I guess there's no bear under my bed."

The "little children" in our churches with weak consciences need love, truth and exercise.

Ephesians 4:15 gives us the recipe: "Speaking the truth in love." Love without truth is hypocrisy, but truth without love is brutality. We don't want either extreme. If you have knowledge without love, that's tyranny. If I know something you don't know, I can

40

intimidate you with what I know. But love without knowledge could be anarchy—allowing you to do whatever you want to do. Knowledge and love must be balanced.

In I Corinthians 8 Paul made it very clear that we must never deliberately offend a person's conscience. Conscience attaches itself to the highest standard the person knows. We don't *blame* the person for not knowing more; we *help* the person to know more. We open the Word of God and teach him.

Romans 14 and 15 give us three instructions for helping those who have a weak conscience. First, receive them. "Him that is weak in the faith receive ye" (14:1). Don't argue with them, receive them. Don't argue about music, translations or worldliness, just receive them. And receive them in love! Don't judge one another. Don't condemn one another. Learn to be tolerant of one another. A mature person understands that other people can be different. Being different doesn't mean being worse or being better, it just means being different. So receive them.

Second, edify them. Paul told us very clearly in Romans 14:13-23 to edify them, to build them up, to help them grow.

And third, Romans 15 says we should please them. "We, then, that are strong ought to bear the infirmities of the weak, and not to please ourselves" (v. 1). A little baby is catered to. The baby is pleased (not pampered, not spoiled), and the parents give in to the baby. Why? The baby lacks understanding

41

and needs a time of transition, an opportunity for growth.

Why do we receive the person who has a weak conscience? That we might be able to edify him. Why do we please him? That we might be able to edify him. Why do we share the truth in love? That we might help him grow out of a weak conscience into a strong conscience.

I think the mistake we're making in our churches today is that we receive people who have a weak conscience *and then we keep them that way!* That is unbiblical! We must help them to grow. Romans 14 makes it very clear that our task is to love them, to please them and to receive them—not so that we can argue with them and judge them but to help them grow so they, in turn, can help other Christians grow.

I think that many of the problems in churches today are caused by people who have a weak conscience. They are critical, they are easily offended, they are unstable, they lack knowledge. It's tragic when these people get into places of leadership because then they make everybody else remain babies.

In the home, the older children help the younger children grow up. When we have in our church a Christian with a weak conscience, it's our job to help that person to grow up. It's a marvelous thing when we have this mixture of strong and weak in our churches because those who have the weak conscience remind those who are stronger not to be arrogant and proud but to be tender, loving and patient. Those who have a strong conscience are to help those with a weak conscience grow up.

May the Lord help us not to have a weak conscience but to grow in Him, to have a strong conscience and to help others grow and be strong in the Lord.

Chapter 5

A Strong Conscience

We have considered the *weak* conscience, and now we want to think about the *strong* conscience. In Romans 14 and 15 Paul dealt with a conflict among the people in the church—some had weak consciences and some had strong consciences.

Paul began by saying, "Him that is weak in the faith receive ye, but not to doubtful disputations" (Rom. 14:1). This means, "Don't argue about doubtful things."

The Christian life contains some doubtful areas that good and godly people have disagreed on down through the centuries. The specific details may change from age to age, but the basic problems are the same. What can a Christian do? How far can a Christian go?

In the Roman assembly the problem centered on food and the celebration of special days. The weak Christians would eat only vegetables, while the strong Christians ate all foods. The weak Christians commemorated certain days that were very special to them, while the strong Christians realized that every day was a special day with the Lord. Unfortunately, the weak Christians judged the strong

Christians, and the strong Christians despised the weak Christians.

In Romans 15:1 Paul said, "We, then, that are strong ought to bear the infirmities of the weak, and not to please ourselves." He was talking about being strong in conscience. He was not talking about physical strength but about the spiritual strength that comes when you have a strong conscience.

So the strong conscience is opposed to the weak conscience. Notice that a person can tell when he has a strong conscience. Paul used the word "we" instead of "they": "We, then, that are strong." If you had asked the Apostle Paul, "Paul, are you a man with a strong conscience?" he would have replied, "Yes." Somebody might say, "Well, aren't you being proud?" No, this is not pride at all. If you *know* you have a strong conscience, there's no reason to hide it. If you have a strong conscience, you have some very important responsibilities.

Characteristics of a Strong Conscience

What are the characteristics of a person who has a strong conscience?

Spiritual Knowledge

To begin with, he is *a person with spiritual knowledge.* He knows the Word of God and what it teaches about various matters in the Christian life.

For instance, various kinds of food were a problem in the Roman assemblies. The strong Christian knows that Jesus declared all foods to be clean.

Paul knew that God had made everything good. Peter discovered this same truth on a housetop when he was waiting for his dinner to be prepared (see Acts 10:9-16). He was taught by the Lord that all foods are clean. So the Christian with the strong conscience has spiritual knowledge. He is not living according to superstitions, customs or the Old Testament Law. He's living by New Testament truth. He understands the truth of the Word.

Discernment

Second, *the person with a strong conscience has discernment*. He has exercised his conscience, his spiritual faculties and senses. He knows what is right and wrong and is therefore able to make the right decisions. He exercises his conscience. He's not afraid to obey the Word of God.

Jesus said in John 7:17, "If any man will do his will, he shall know of the doctrine." Obedience results in spiritual knowledge. The person with a strong conscience is discerning because he exercises his spiritual faculties. He steps out by faith and believes and obeys the Word of God.

Enjoyment of Freedom in Christ

This leads us to a third characteristic: *He enjoys his freedom in Christ*. He knows that in Jesus Christ he has freedom, that all things are his and that God gives to us "richly all things to enjoy" (I Tim. 6:17). He realizes that God is a gracious and generous God, that every good gift and every perfect gift comes down from God (see James 1:17).

Therefore, the Christian with a strong conscience appropriates the truth by faith, and he enjoys his freedom.

If you had visited some of the members in the Roman assemblies, you would have seen a contrast between freedom and bondage. The weaker Christians were in bondage. They were living by Old Testament rules and regulations, and consequently they were not enjoying their freedom in Christ. The mature, strong Christians were enjoying their liberty in the Lord because they had appropriated and practiced Bible truths.

Tolerance of Differences in Others

Not only does the person with a strong conscience have spiritual knowledge and spiritual discernment, not only does he enjoy his freedom in the Lord, but *he is tolerant of the differences in others*. This is an important thing. A person with a strong conscience is not easily offended.

We noted that the person with a weak conscience is easily wounded. If somebody does something he doesn't like, he is deeply grieved and offended by it. This is a sign that he has a weak conscience. When a person has a strong conscience, he realizes that good and godly people disagree on some practices, and he does not get offended.

Some years ago a friend of mine was ministering in Scandanavia. He and his interpreter were walking down the street, and my friend began to whistle. His interpreter said to him, "Who is going to preach tonight?" And my friend said, "Well, *I'm* going to preach tonight." The interpreter said, "Oh, no, you can't preach tonight. No, you just grieved the Lord by whistling." Many of the Christians in that part of the world did not believe that people should whistle. Christians would never whistle in public.

At a conference some years ago another friend of mine was chatting with a pastor. This pastor came from a part of the country where the use of tobacco was not frowned upon too much. This pastor was complaining to my friend because the young people were down at the beach together, and he said, "I don't think that you should permit that." My friend reached over and pulled a package of cigarettes from the man's pocket and said, "Well, you take care of this, and we'll take care of that!"

What was he saying to him? He was saying, "Brother, there is such a thing as geographical Christianity. In some parts of the world some things are frowned upon that may be approved in other parts of the world."

You may say, "But isn't that rather inconsistent?" No, not at all. The Christian who has a strong conscience realizes that good and godly people can disagree on practice. We aren't talking about *doctrine.* The fundamentals of the faith are true regardless of whether you are in Asia, Africa, Australia or America. But practices have a way of changing with culture. We're talking about this area of questionable things. The Christian who has a strong conscience is tolerant of differences. He realizes that differences do not necessarily mean that one person is better or worse than the other. You will notice changes as you go from place to place and from culture to culture. The person with a strong conscience is not easily offended. The strong believer doesn't stumble and get hurt. He doesn't sit and nurse his wounds. He doesn't get critical. The Christian with a strong conscience enjoys his freedom and is willing to give that same freedom to others.

Responsibilities of the Strong Christian

But the strong Christian also has some responsibilities. Romans 14 and 15 were written to the strong Christian primarily, and these chapters state our responsibilities if we claim to have a strong Christian conscience.

Receive the Weak

Our first responsibility is to *receive the weak.* "Him that is weak in the faith, receive ye, but not to doubtful disputations [questionable things]" (Rom. 14:1). We are not to keep people out of the church fellowship because they haven't grown up yet. The church is God's nursery for helping babies to grow. We have the responsibility of receiving the Christian who has the weaker conscience.

Do Not Argue

Second, we have the responsibility *not to argue with him.* I would strongly advise you not to argue with people about these areas where you disagree. We can discuss principles, we can discuss biblical

49

doctrine; but in areas of taste and custom, there is simply no way to agree.

Do Not Despise the Weak

Third, those who are strong are *not to despise those who are weak*. Romans 14:3 says, "Let not him that eateth despise him that eateth not; and let not him who eateth not judge him that eateth." In other words, the strong Christian is not to despise the weak Christian, and the weak Christian is not supposed to condemn the strong Christian because he enjoys his freedom.

Do Not Cause the Weak to Stumble

Fourth, and this is very important, the strong Christian is *not to cause the weak Christian to stumble*. Romans 14:13 says, "Let us not, therefore, judge one another any more; but judge this, rather: that no man put a stumbling block or an occasion to fall in his brother's way."

This brings us to what Paul wrote in I Corinthians 8, 9 and 10. The problem in Corinth was, If you are invited to a feast at the local temple, should you go? After all, that's an idol's temple, and that meat was offered to an idol. Paul said it may not hurt *you*, but it might hurt your weaker brother. If your brother sees you in that temple, he may be tempted to go against his conscience, and you will cause him to stumble. I can do many things that may not hurt *me*, but they might hurt somebody else.

We are not to cause the weak to stumble. We are not to grieve our weaker brother by our liberty.

Romans 14:15 says, "But if thy brother be grieved with thy food, now walkest thou not in love." We should walk to please our weaker brother, not to please ourselves. "Let every one of us please his neighbor for his good to edification" (15:2).

You may say, "Well, why should I give up my liberty just to please my brother?" Because that's Christian love. Why should you use your freedom to cause somebody else to stumble? We have to be very careful how we handle these matters. We should walk in love.

Make Peace

The stronger Christian has another responsibility: *He should make peace.* "Let us, therefore, follow after the things which make for peace" (Rom. 14:19). Some Christians are forever declaring war! They are constantly looking down on people they feel are inferior to them. Paul said, "Don't do that. Do the things that result in peace. What difference does it make whether you eat meat or don't eat meat? The important thing is that your brother and you get along. An unsaved world is watching. Don't be caught fighting one another."

Not only should we make peace, but we should build up the weaker brother. We should do those things that help to edify others. The reason we receive the weaker brother and seek to please him is that we might help him grow up.

You cannot force your faith on somebody else. "Hast thou faith? Have it to thyself before God" (v. 22). You cannot push truth down someone's throat and force them to digest it! We have to speak the truth in love (Eph. 4:15). We must demonstrate patience, love and kindness if we are to help these people grow.

The important thing is for the stronger Christians not to abuse their freedom. In Romans 15 Paul used the Lord Jesus Christ as our example: "For even Christ pleased not himself" (v. 3). Think of the freedom that Jesus deprived Himself of so that He might help others! He was the perfect Son of God who knew all things, and yet He deliberately humbled Himself, He deliberately limited Himself so that He might be able to minister to us. The result, of course, brought glory to God.

"Wherefore, receive ye one another, as Christ also received us to the glory of God" (v. 7). That settles the matter right there. The weak Christian is not to break fellowship with the stronger Christian over such things as amusements, food, Bible translations, different kinds of music or methods of teaching. It is so easy for the weaker Christian to feel threatened, to get defensive and to say, "I can't fellowship here any more. These people do too many things that are wrong." He never will grow up if he has that attitude. However, if the strong Christians have an attitude of superiority, there will be trouble in the church.

In I Corinthians 8:9 Paul warned, "But take heed lest by any means this liberty of yours become a stumbling block to them that are weak." I have the right to enjoy my freedom, but I also have the freedom to give up my rights. That's a part of my freedom in the Lord. I have the right to enjoy all things that God has created. But if, in using that freedom, I rob you of blessing or I hurt you, then it isn't freedom at all. It has become bondage. Those who are strong in the Lord must be very careful not to look down on those who have not matured. However, those who have not yet grown in the Lord ought to start growing. There ought to be such an atmosphere of love, knowledge and acceptance in the church that the weakest Christian can receive the Word of God and grow.

I suppose you can summarize it by saying that we belong to each other, we affect each other, and we need each other. The strong Christian needs the weak Christian, and the weak Christian needs the strong Christian. We all need the Lord. If we live to please ourselves and to boast about our knowledge and our freedom, then we will cause division, dissension and destruction in the church. But if we live to please the Lord Jesus and to please one another, if we show preference to those who are weaker, then we are going to help them grow. At the same time, we are going to grow, and there will be a beautiful atmosphere of love in the church. The spiritual babies will grow up and help other babies grow up. God's work will progress, and Jesus Christ will be glorified!

Chapter 6

An Evil Conscience

Have you ever wondered how it's possible for people to do evil things and not be bothered about them? Some people can lie and never lose any sleep. They can steal and do other evil things, and it never seems to upset them. But you and I are bothered by even a little thing until we come to the Lord and get it straightened out. How can some people do evil things and not be disturbed? The answer may be that they have an evil conscience.

"Let us draw near with a true heart in full assurance of faith, having our hearts sprinkled from an evil conscience, and our bodies washed with pure water" (Heb. 10:22). The writer used Old Testament symbolism to convey a New Testament truth. When the priest was ministering in the tabernacle, he had to wash his hands and his feet at the laver so he would not defile the tabernacle. You and I, when we fellowship with the Lord, must be sure that we are washed clean. "Create in me a clean heart, O God, and renew a right spirit within me" (Ps. 51:10). "Behold, thou desirest truth in the inward parts" (v. 6).

What Is an Evil Conscience?

Let's try to understand this concept of an evil conscience by answering several questions. First of all, *what is an evil conscience?* The simplest explanation I think is simply this: An evil conscience is the opposite of a good conscience. A good conscience is effective—it convicts us when we have done wrong, and it encourages us when we have done right. But an evil conscience encourages the person when he does wrong and bothers him if he does something right!

I think Isaiah 5:20 describes people who have an evil conscience: "Woe unto them that call evil, good, and good, evil; who put darkness for light, and light for darkness; who put bitter for sweet, and sweet for bitter!"

In other words, they brag about the things they ought to be ashamed of. Paul wrote about them in Philippians 3:19: "Whose glory is in their shame, who mind earthly things." The things they ought to be ashamed of, they glory in! When they do something good, it disturbs them. Why? Because they don't want to do good, they want to do evil. When they do something to hurt someone else, it doesn't bother them because their inner light has turned into darkness.

This takes us again to Matthew 6 where the Lord Jesus compared conscience to a window that lets in the light: "The lamp of the body is the eye; if, therefore, thine eye be healthy, thy whole body shall be full of light. But if thine eye be evil, thy whole body shall be full of darkness" (v. 22,23). Note this important statement: "If, therefore, the light that is in thee be darkness, how great is that darkness!" (v. 23).

Conscience is the window that lets in the light. As we sin against the Lord, that window gets dirtier and dirtier. Finally, the light doesn't disappear, *the light turns into darkness!* That which should guide us into truth guides us into error. This is an awesome thing. Jesus did not say that, as we continue to sin, the light disappears. No, He said a far worse fate will overtake us: The light will turn into darkness! That which should be a blessing to us becomes a curse. That which should help us begins to hurt us.

So an evil conscience is one that calls evil, good and good, evil. It puts darkness for light and light for darkness. An evil conscience does not convict us when we have done wrong. We get accustomed to our sins, and our conscience does not bother us.

What Causes an Evil Conscience?

What causes an evil conscience? I think the simple answer to that question is this: *a failure to be serious about sin.* It is dangerous to take sin lightly. If I can, without feeling guilty, do something today that six months ago would have bothered me, then I may be starting to get an evil conscience. When you start to take sin lightly, you are moving in the wrong direction—from light to darkness.

I think one reason why many people today take sin so lightly is that they take God very lightly. When we do not have a holy respect for God, then

56

we have no respect for holiness or for God's judgment of sin.

In I John 1, John talked about people who try to cover their sin. He pointed out that they cover sin with their speech. "If we say that we have fellowship with him, and walk in darkness, we lie, and do not the truth" (v. 6). They begin to lie to other people. They say, "Oh, yes, I'm in fellowship with God." They sing the songs and give their testimonies, but they're walking in the darkness.

In I John 1:8 we see them start to lie to themselves: "If we say that we have no sin, we deceive ourselves, and the truth is not in us." They can tell the same lie so often that they really start to believe it! First John 1:10 says, "If we say that we have not sinned, we make him a liar, and his word is not in us." Next they lie to God! They might go through a form of prayer, but they aren't really praying. It is all a masquerade.

A good conscience functions properly. But if we sin against that good conscience, we develop a defiled conscience. "Unto the pure all things are pure, but unto them that are defiled and unbelieving is nothing pure; but even their mind and conscience is defiled" (Titus 1:15). A good conscience becomes defiled because the window starts to get dirty. The more we sin against the Lord, the dirtier that window becomes.

This can lead to a *seared* conscience. "Speaking lies in hypocrisy, having their conscience seared with a hot iron" (I Tim. 4:2). This image is not difficult to understand. When your skin is burned, it develops a calloused area of scar tissue, and that area loses its sensitivity. In a similar manner your conscience can be seared.

First, a good conscience becomes a defiled conscience, and then a defiled conscience becomes a seared conscience. It's possible to get to such a low point in our lives that sin doesn't bother us anymore. We can lie with a straight face, and it doesn't bother us one bit. This, of course, leads to an evil conscience.

What Are the Evidences of an Evil Conscience?

Someone may ask, "How can I know if I have an evil conscience?" Let me give you some evidences of an evil conscience.

Playing With Sin

The first evidence is that *you play with sin.* Whenever you start playing with sin, you don't take it seriously. The person with an evil conscience can play with sin and not be worried.

Shallow Confession and Shallow Repentance

Another evidence is *shallow confession and shallow repentance.* Whenever I make excuses instead of confessing my sin to God, I know something is wrong inside. The person with an evil conscience can make very shallow confessions and very hasty repentance that is not repentance at all—he's just making excuses.

58

Measuring Sin

I think another evidence of an evil conscience is that *we start to measure sin*. We try to convince ourselves that there are big sins and little sins. In God's sight sin is sin, and the more understanding we have, the more we'll realize that what we thought were small sins are just as bad as the so-called big sins in our lives. Someone may say, "Well, I haven't murdered anybody. That's a big sin. I've not committed adultery. Therefore, I can get away with these smaller sins."

The British Bible teacher, Dr. G. Campbell Morgan, used to talk about "sins in good standing." I fear that in our churches today there are sins in good standing. We would expel a member for fornication or drunkenness or murder, but what about gossip? What about lying? What about pride? The person with an evil conscience measures sin—he classifies some sins as big and some as little.

Concerned About Reputation

A person with an evil conscience is *more concerned about reputation than about character*. If you have an evil conscience, all you are concerned about is that you don't get caught. And even if you do get caught, you can talk your way out of it! People who are more concerned about reputation than about character will do anything privately if they aren't caught or seen publicly. What a dangerous attitude this is because your conscience begins to decay and become evil.

59

Arguing With the Truth

I think another evidence of an evil conscience is that *we start to argue with the truth.* When you meet a Christian who is supersensitive about some matter, watch out! He may be developing an evil conscience. You can't talk to him about the subject because he's already made up his mind. He can argue with the truth. He can explain away what he's doing. I have even known professing Christians who used the Bible to support their sin.

Who Can Get an Evil Conscience?

We've asked the questions, What is an evil conscience, what causes an evil conscience and what are the evidences of an evil conscience? Here's another question: *Can this happen to anyone?* Yes, it can happen to you, and it can happen to me.

It happened to King Saul. I think one of the most tragic biographies in the Bible is that of King Saul. He started off with such great blessings—anointed with the Spirit, surrounded by a group of men who wanted to work with him. He faced great opportunity. He had a marvelous friend, Samuel, who prayed for him. But then Saul got impatient, and he began to lie. He was worried about impressing people. He said to Samuel, "Honor me before the people" (see I Sam. 15:30). He became envious of David. And he ended up in the darkness of a witches' cave because God had forsaken him (see 28:7-25). Then he went to the battlefield and committed suicide (see 31:1-6).

It all started when Saul lied to his conscience and played around with sin. King Saul went down into darkness because he had an evil conscience. Those who were his best friends, he treated like enemies. Those who were really his enemies, he treated like friends.

But I would remind you that this also happened to David. In I Samuel 24 we read that David cut off the skirt of King Saul's robe when the king was asleep. And this bothered David. The Bible says, "David's heart smote him" (v. 5). David's conscience at this point was so tender that this little action upset him. In I Samuel 26 he took the spear and the water jug from Saul, but we don't read that his heart smote him when he did it. A few years later David took Bathsheba and murdered her husband, and for a whole year he covered his sin! Was it possible for the sweet singer of Israel to get an evil conscience? Yes! It happened to David and Saul, and it can happen *to you and me!*

Can an Evil Conscience Be Cured?

This brings us to our final question: *Can an evil conscience be cured?* The answer is *yes*. We can come to the Lord and have our hearts cleansed from an evil conscience. First of all, we must confess the sin honestly before God and demonstrate an attitude of true repentance. David, in Psalm 51, gave us a beautiful illustration of how to be broken before God. We need to be cleansed and purged by the blood of the Lord Jesus Christ.

"How much more shall the blood of Christ, who through the eternal Spirit offered himself without spot to God, purge your conscience from dead works to serve the living God?" (Heb. 9:14). We must truly repent of our sin and confess it to God. We must repair any damage we can through restitution or apology. We must be cleansed and purged of our guilt. We must also draw near to God. "Let us draw near . . . in full assurance of faith, having our hearts sprinkled from an evil conscience" (10:22). The author of the Book of Hebrews was talking about cleansing by the blood of the Lord Jesus Christ.

If, in honesty, someone says, "I have an evil conscience," I would warn him: Not only will your light turn into darkness, but you will also cause other people to live in darkness. The tragedy of having an evil conscience is the damage that we do to other people. The husband who has an evil conscience will do damage to his wife and his family. The teenager who has an evil conscience will do damage to his parents and his friends. Think of the damage Saul and David caused.

Is there something in our lives today that we are afraid might be found out? Are we cultivating an evil conscience, being more concerned about reputation than about character? Are we more concerned about what people think we are than about what God knows we really are?

I would issue this warning: If you live with an evil conscience, ultimately it will destroy you. It may not kill you the way it killed King Saul, but it can destroy your joy, your power, your fellowship with God, your character. It will destroy your peace. It will destroy your fellowship with those who love you.

But I can say to you on the authority of the Word of God, no matter how dark your conscience may be, if you will come to Jesus Christ and confess your sin in an attitude of true repentance, He will restore you. He will cleanse you. He will wash the window of your soul, and the light will start to shine in again. Then you will want to be very careful to maintain a sensitive conscience, being obedient to God's will.

May the Lord help each one of us maintain a good conscience, lest we develop a defiled conscience and then an evil conscience!

Chapter 7

Conscience and Ministry

Conscience is important for Christian living. It is also important for Christian service. What Paul wrote to Timothy in I Timothy 1:19 must be taken to heart by all of us who serve Jesus Christ: "Holding faith, and a good conscience." It's much easier to hold to the faith and to be evangelical and orthodox in theology than it is to have a good conscience. It is unfortunate that occasionally bad publicity is given to some Christian worker who was true to the faith but who didn't have a good conscience. As a result, he got into trouble.

Conscience is important if we are going to be effective in our ministry. Let's look at five different areas of ministry where conscience is vitally important.

Winning the Lost

First of all, conscience is important in the area of *winning the lost*. After all, that's why we're in the world—to win the lost to Jesus Christ.

Romans 9:1-3 says, "I say the truth in Christ, I lie not, my conscience also bearing me witness in the Holy Spirit, that I have great heaviness and continual sorrow in my heart. For I could wish that I myself were accursed from Christ for my brethren, my kinsmen according to the flesh."

The Apostle Paul had a great burden to reach his own people, the Israelites. Even though Paul was called to be a missionary to the Gentiles, he always had a burden for the Jewish nation. Paul's burden was a *real* burden, not an artificial burden.

I trust that I will not be misunderstood as I say this, but I fear that sometimes soul winning, or witnessing, becomes a fad. Some preachers and teachers make soul winning a "Gospel hobby." They are forever counting how many they witness to or how many they win to Christ. And I think this is wrong. I think it's good to be able to report statistics. Mr. Spurgeon used to say that those who criticize statistics usually have none to report. I see nothing wrong with praising God for people who have been won. But only God knows how many of them are true believers. The important thing is not the report; the important thing is your motivation.

Paul's burden was real, not artificial. He said, "My conscience also bearing me witness" (v. 1). The Holy Spirit witnessed to the fact that Paul had a sincere love for lost souls. We need that same love today.

It's very easy for me as a preacher to preach something from the Bible that I don't really feel in my own heart, and that's dangerous. It's possible for Sunday school teachers to teach a lesson to their students that has no meaning for them at all. It's possible even for us to witness to people simply out of obligation and not because of true concern or love for them.

Peter had something to say about this in I Peter 3:15,16: "But sanctify the Lord God in your hearts [sanctify Christ as Lord in your hearts], and be ready always to give an answer to every man that asketh you a reason of the hope that is in you, with meekness and fear, having a good conscience, that, whereas they speak evil of you, as of evildoers, they may be ashamed that falsely accuse your good manner of life in Christ."

We must have a good conscience as we witness. If we don't have a good conscience, we will have no power in our witness. If, while I'm sharing the Gospel with others, I know that in my own heart something is wrong, God cannot bless.

Planning for Service

The second area where we must have a good conscience if we're going to minister effectively is in *making our plans for service*. In II Corinthians 1:12 we read: "For our rejoicing is this, the testimony of our conscience, that in simplicity and godly sincerity, not with fleshly wisdom but by the grace of God, we have behaved ourselves in the world, and more abundantly toward you."

Let me give a bit of background here. Paul had promised to come to Corinth and perhaps even spend the winter with them. He was going to take up a collection for the poor Jews in Jerusalem. Paul made his plans and shared them with the Corinthians, and then he had to change his plans. The church accused Paul of being devious and of not meaning what he said. They said, "When Paul says yes, he means no, and when Paul says no, he means yes." Paul spent several chapters in II Corinthians straightening out this disagreement and misunderstanding.

I have had to cancel meetings. I have received letters from people who have been upset with me because circumstances forced me to change my plans. I recall that, when my mother had a stroke and I had to change all my plans, a few people where I was to speak in conferences were very unhappy because I had to rearrange my plans.

At times I have said to people, "I'd like very much to come and minister," and then God has changed my plans. The important thing is that you have a good conscience.

We make plans and say, "If the Lord wills, we'll do thus and so." We can't guarantee that this is what God wants us to do. We don't always know every detail about the will of God for our service. The important thing is for us not to scheme and lie but to be open and honest. Paul said, "My conscience testifies to me that I was sincere. I had integrity. I was not using fleshly wisdom. I'm sorry it didn't work out the way you wanted it to work out, but my conscience bears witness that I was not wrong."

Someone has said that faith means living without scheming. If you start scheming in your ministry, watch out! You're not living by faith.

67

Ministering God's Word

The third area of ministry where conscience is important is *in the ministry of the Word of God.* Second Corinthians 4:2 says, "But [we] have renounced the hidden things of dishonesty, not walking in craftiness, nor handling the word of God deceitfully, but by manifestation of the truth commending ourselves to every man's conscience in the sight of God."

Second Corinthians 5:11 says, "Knowing, therefore, the terror of the Lord, we persuade men; but we are made manifest unto God, and I trust also are made manifest in your consciences."

Paul was saying two things here: When we minister the Word of God, our conscience is open before God. Our conscience is also open before people. At times when I have heard an individual sharing the Word of God, my conscience has begun to bother me because he was not handling the Word of God accurately. Paul was telling us that, as we share the Word of God, we ought to have a conscience void of offense before God and before people.

Some people deliberately twist the Word of God; they use dishonesty and craftiness. Some have schemes whereby they can prove anything from the Bible. But when you use the Word of God honestly, when you use the Word of God with a clear conscience, then God can bless.

If I am ministering the Word of God and my conscience is open before you and before God, then the Spirit can use the Word and bless your life.

But if I'm being deceitful and crafty, if I'm handling the Word of God in some devious way, then it's impossible for God to bless. Unfortunately, many people don't know the difference—they listen to a speaker and do not know whether or not he's using the Word of God accurately. If your conscience is functioning as it should, the Holy Spirit of God will give you discernment.

Not only should we be honest in ministering God's Word, *but we should practice what we preach.* It's easier to preach than it is to practice. In I Timothy 3:9,10, Paul wrote to the deacons: "Holding the mystery of the faith in a pure conscience. And let these also first be proved; then let them use the office of a deacon, being found blameless." Proved in what way? Let them prove that they practice what they believe. "Holding the mystery of the faith in a pure conscience." In other words, we should not be orthodox in belief only but also orthodox in behavior. It is important that we have a good conscience as we minister God's Word, not twisting the Word of God, not making the Word of God say something it doesn't say. No preacher or Sunday school teacher should prepare a sermon or a lesson and then try to find a Scripture passage to fit it. Go to the Word of God first and find out what it says. Then prepare the message or the Sunday school lesson.

Facing Criticism

Conscience is important in our ministry, not only in winning the lost, in making our plans for service and in ministering God's Word but also *in facing criticism.*

First Corinthians 4:1-5 says, "Let a man so account of us, as of the ministers of Christ, and stewards of the mysteries of God. Moreover, it is required in stewards, that a man be found faithful. But with me it is a very small thing that I should be judged of you, or of man's judgment; yea, I judge not mine own self. For I know nothing against myself, yet am I not hereby justified; but he that judgeth me is the Lord. Therefore, judge nothing before the time, until the Lord come, who both will bring to light the hidden things of darkness, and will make manifest the counsels of the hearts; and then shall every man have praise of God."

Paul was severely criticized by the Corinthian church. They compared him with Peter and with Apollos. They said that Paul was a dynamic letter writer but a very boring preacher. They had a lot of criticism against Paul and his ministry. Paul said, in effect, "The criticism doesn't bother me. Men can criticize me. I don't even criticize myself." The word translated "know" that he used in the phrase "I know nothing against myself" (or "I know nothing by myself") comes from the same root as the Greek word for conscience. He was saying, "My conscience does not accuse me." Then he added, "Yet am I not hereby justified." In other words, it's possible to have a clear conscience and still be wrong. But Paul was saying, "When you face criticism and you know you are right, your conscience gives you strength, and you can take it."

70

Years ago Dr. A. W. Tozer taught a good lesson. He said, "Never be afraid of honest criticism because it can help somebody. If the person who criticizes you is wrong, you can help him. If he's right, he can help you." So honest criticism can be helpful. But sometimes in the ministry there's a lot of dishonest and malicious criticism and a lot of complaining. Paul said, in effect, "If your conscience is clear, you can take it because the Lord is with you."

Opposing False Doctrine

A final area where we must use conscience wisely as we minister is *in opposing false doctrine.*

First Timothy 1:18,19 says, "This charge I commit unto thee, son Timothy, according to the prophecies which pointed to thee, that thou by them [the prophecies] mightest war a good warfare, holding faith, and a good conscience, which some, having put away concerning faith, have made shipwreck."

How do you fight the battle against false doctrine? With faith and a good conscience, with the Word of God and a good conscience. We have to be orthodox in our theology, and we also have to be orthodox in our living. Some people think they can battle against the lies of the Devil even though they have a bad conscience. I want you to know that when the Devil finds a defiled conscience, he makes a beachhead there. Satan likes nothing better than to find a Christian worker who's not practicing what he preaches. Satan won't stop him from *preaching*

71

the truth, just as long as he does not *live* the truth. That is what happened to King Saul. He began gradually to move away from the truth of the Word of God, and finally he ended up in ruin and in disgrace.

The Devil can use an orthodox preacher to further his cause by wrecking the preacher's testimony. Nothing can do more damage than a good man who falls into bad living.

Conscience is a mighty weapon for fighting false doctrine and fighting the battles of the Lord.

Recently I have been rereading a biography of Martin Luther, the great reformer, and he said this when he was on trial: "Unless therefore I am convinced by the testimony of Scripture, or by the clearest reasoning—unless I am persuaded by means of the passages I have quoted—and unless they thus render my conscience bound by the Word of God, I cannot and I will not retract, for it is unsafe for a Christian to speak against his conscience. Here I stand, I can do no other; May God help me! Amen!"

How could this man stand against nations and religious leaders and have that kind of courage? He had a good conscience. When your conscience is bound by the Word of God, then you can courageously oppose false doctrine.

We have discussed five areas of ministry where conscience is vitally important. If we are going to win the lost, our conscience must testify that we have a sincere burden for people. We aren't out just to win converts and count numbers. If we are making plans for ministry, our conscience must witness that we are not scheming and trying to promote our own selfish purposes. As we minister God's Word, our conscience must testify that we're not twisting the Word of God or handling it in some deceptive way. As we face criticism (and all of us face it), we must be sure that our conscience is clear. If the critic is right, he can help us. If he's wrong, he can't hurt us. Our conscience bears witness that we're serving the Lord. Finally, as we fight the battles of the Lord and oppose false doctrine, conscience is a mighty weapon to give us victory.

What is the condition of your conscience today? Would it not be good for all of us to go before the Lord and find out from Him if we have a good conscience, a conscience void of offense, a pure conscience? If we have a good conscience, we can minister effectively to the glory of God.

Chapter 8

Conscience and Government

As Christians our citizenship is in heaven, but we are also citizens of this world. We may be pilgrims and strangers walking through this world, but we still must relate to people around us and to civil government.

The classic chapter in the New Testament on the Christian and government is Romans 13: "Let every soul be subject unto the higher powers. For there is no power but of God; the powers that be are ordained of God" (v. 1). Paul stated here that authority has been established by God. And he went on to say in this chapter that there are four reasons why the Christian ought to obey government: to avoid wrath or punishment (vv. 1-4); for conscience' sake (vv. 5-7); for love's sake because love is the fulfillment of the law (vv. 8-10); and for Jesus' sake because the coming of the Lord is near (vv. 11-14).

I want us to focus on verse 5 where he says we should be subject for conscience' sake. Is it ever right for a Christian, for conscience' sake, to disobey the government? The answer is yes, *but we* must be very careful how we do this. There is such a thing as Christian civil disobedience, but we must be very careful as Christians how we function in this area.

Biblical Examples

Let's begin first of all with some biblical examples of people who did defy the government although they showed respect for the authority.

Jewish Midwives, Moses' Parents

According to Exodus 1, some Jewish midwives were commanded by Pharaoh to kill all the boy babies born to the Jewish mothers. They refused to do it, and as a consequence, they had to answer for that. They practiced civil disobedience. They respected the government even though they disobeyed what they thought was a wrong law. Moses' parents also refused to obey the same law (see Heb. 11:23).

Daniel and His Friends

Daniel, of course, also comes to mind. According to Daniel 1, Daniel refused to eat the food that was put before him. I appreciate the gracious way that Daniel took care of this problem. He did not make a nuisance of himself. He did not try to intimidate the man who was in charge. Rather, he tried as much as possible to live peaceably with all men. He refused to eat the food that had been offered to idols, food that no dedicated Jew could eat. He disobeyed the

Law even though he showed respect for the government.

In Daniel 6 we read that a law was passed forbidding the people to pray or to make a request of anyone except the king for 30 days. Daniel, of course, broke that law. He had his regular times of prayer, and he was arrested for it and thrown into the lions' den. You'll recall, of course, that God delivered him from the lions' den and honored His name through Daniel. Daniel respected the authority, but he did not obey the law.

The three Hebrew men refused to bow down to Nebuchadnezzar's image, and as a result, they were thrown into the fiery furnace (see Dan. 3). They practiced civil disobedience. They respected the government, but they did not obey what they knew was a wrong law.

Jeremiah

When you read the Book of Jeremiah, you discover that the Prophet Jeremiah regularly was disobedient to the government. For example, he said that the city should surrender to the Babylonians. People called Jeremiah a traitor to the Jewish nation. Imagine, surrendering to the Babylonians! But this was the message God had given him. Jeremiah refused to go along with the politics of his day. He refused to promote the alliances that the unbelieving king was making as he tried to solve his political problem. Jeremiah was considered a traitor. He was arrested and was put in the dungeon, and yet Jeremiah stood true to the Word of God.

Peter and the Other Apostles

I suppose the greatest example in the New Testament is that of Peter and the other apostles. In Acts 4 they were arrested, and they stood before the Sanhedrin to give their testimony. "But Peter and John answered and said unto them, Whether it is right in the sight of God to hearken unto you more than unto God, judge ye. For we cannot but speak the things which we have seen and heard" (vv. 19,20). "Then Peter and the other apostles answered, and said, We ought to obey God rather than men" (5:29). They showed respect for the government, but they did not obey the law.

These are examples from the Bible of people who practiced what is known today as civil disobedience. That title comes from an essay that was written by Henry David Thoreau, the American naturalist. He refused to pay his poll tax because he would not support the Mexican War, and so he spent one night in the Concord, Massachusetts, jail. He inaugurated this thing called "civil disobedience." Gandhi read that essay, and it helped him in his battle for freedom in India. Many of the modern civil rights leaders have followed the principles of Thoreau in practicing civil disobedience.

Principles to Follow

Let's gather some basic principles from these examples for us to follow. Knowing the principles is very important.

Total Control

If you are going to practice civil disobedience, be sure that your conscience controls *all of your life and not just one area.*

I read about university students who refuse to go into the army because of conscience. But their conscience doesn't bother them when they get drunk. Their conscience doesn't bother them when they wreck an automobile at high speed. Their conscience doesn't bother them when they cheat on examinations. I have a hard time believing a person is conscientious about war when he is not conscientious about anything else.

And so the first principle is this: Conscience must control *all of our lives* if we are going to practice civil disobedience. If I see someone who has a good conscience, someone who's walking with God, someone whose conscience guides him day by day, and that person refuses to go to battle, I would accept it. I would believe that he is conscientiously objecting to bearing arms and being honest about it.

It may interest you to know that D. L. Moody, the great evangelist, probably would have been a conscientious objector. He said he simply could not bear arms. Many people, for conscience' sake, will not go to war. They will help in other ways—in the hospital, for example—but they will not bear arms.

If your conscience controls *all of your life* and you're seeking to glorify God, then you can practice civil disobedience.

Biblical Conviction

Second, you must base your disobedience on *biblical conviction*. In other words, you are disobeying human law because you are obeying God's law. The midwives knew that they should not kill. Therefore, they obeyed God, not people. Daniel knew he could not eat food that was prohibited to the Jews. Daniel knew he could not pray to a man instead of to God. The Word of God makes it very clear that idolatry is wrong. The three Hebrew men who were thrown into the furnace knew it was wrong to bow down to an idol. They had definite biblical convictions.

The apostles had been *commanded* to preach, beginning in Jerusalem. They had definite biblical authority behind their convictions.

There are areas in politics and government where good and godly people disagree. Don't make these areas a test of fellowship or spirituality. If you have a biblical conviction about a matter, then that's fine—you hold to it—but don't force your convictions on other people. Good and godly people disagree on some areas. But on the broad areas of life the Word of God is very clear. It's wrong to murder, it's wrong to steal, it's wrong to bow down to idols.

Courtesy

It takes courage to practice civil disobedience, but *be sure you practice courtesy with your courage.* I am impressed with the fact that each of these persons in the Bible who practiced civil disobedience showed courtesy, kindness and love. They were not burning down buildings. They were not militantly calling people names. In fact, they did just the opposite. They went the extra mile to try to work these matters out in a respectful way. It is possible to respect the authority and still disobey the law. It is possible to be obedient to God and still be disobedient to people.

Daniel could have gotten his guard into trouble. Instead, Daniel said, "Let's try my diet out for ten days. If, at the end of ten days, it doesn't work, we'll work something else out." Daniel had no right to get his guard into trouble. You have no right to get somebody else into trouble because of your convictions. We must respect other people's convictions as well.

I think this is why Paul urged us to pray for those in authority. "I exhort, therefore, that first of all, supplications, prayers, intercessions, and giving of thanks, be made for all men, for kings, and for all that are in authority, that we may lead a quiet and peaceable life in all godliness and honesty" (I Tim. 2:1,2).

Opportunity for Witnessing

If you're going to practice civil disobedience, *be sure it provides an opportunity to witness.* This is important. We aren't just opposing some bad law, we are seeking to glorify God. Everything we do as Christians affects how people view the Bible. It affects what people think of Christians. It affects their attitude toward the Gospel. I must ask myself,

"When I'm all through with this battle, will it be easier to win people to Christ? Will it be easier to witness to them? Will God be glorified?"

Titus 3:1,2 says, "Put them in mind to be subject to principalities and powers, to obey magistrates, to be ready to every good work, to speak evil of no man, to be no brawlers, but gentle, showing all meekness unto all men." That's hard to do, but it's easy to understand. When those who claim to be practicing civil disobedience are brawling and fighting with malice and meanness, I have a hard time believing it comes from a godly conscience. We should look for opportunities to witness.

The Jewish midwives brought glory to God. Daniel was able to bring glory to God. The apostles brought glory to God, and people were saved because of the way they behaved. I fear that some civil disobedience is just plain meanness coming out of people's hearts. They just don't like the government, and so they use conscience as a cover-up for their own maliciousness.

Example of Christ

Follow the example of Christ. First Peter 2:13-25 makes it very clear that Jesus was meek and lowly, that He committed Himself to those who were abusing Him and that He took it patiently for conscience' sake. Peter wrote: "Submit yourselves to every ordinance of man for the Lord's sake, whether it be to the king, as supreme, or unto governors. . . . For so is the will of God, that with well-doing ye may put

81

to silence the ignorance of foolish men" (vv. 13-15). We're not supposed to have a big mouth and clenched fists—we're supposed to follow the example of Christ.

The Lord Jesus lost *all* of His civil rights. Herod didn't help Him, Pilate didn't help Him, the Jewish priests didn't help Him. Jesus was under three different jurisdictions—Herod, Pilate and the Sanhedrin. He lost His civil rights, and yet He meekly served and obeyed His Father. We should follow the example of Christ.

Obligations and Peacemaking

Let me share two concluding remarks: First, we are supposed to render to Caesar the things that are Caesar's (Matt. 22:15-22). We have certain obligations. I appreciate police protection and fire protection. I appreciate the streets I drive on. I appreciate city government. I should therefore take my share of the responsibility. We should give to Caesar the things that are Caesar's and to God the things that are God's. And when they conflict, we must serve God first, but let's be sure we're doing it God's way on the basis of His Word.

Second, Romans 12:18 says, "If it be possible, as much as lieth in you, live peaceably with all men." Sometimes it isn't possible, but if it is possible, we must make peace. I think Paul was suggesting in Romans 12:18 that, before you become militant, you try the peaceful solution. That's what Daniel did. That's what the apostles did. If *others* declare war, we can't help that. We ought to obey God rather than people, but let's be careful that as we obey God we also glorify God. When we practice true Christian civil disobedience, God will get the glory.